GUILDFORD

A Short History

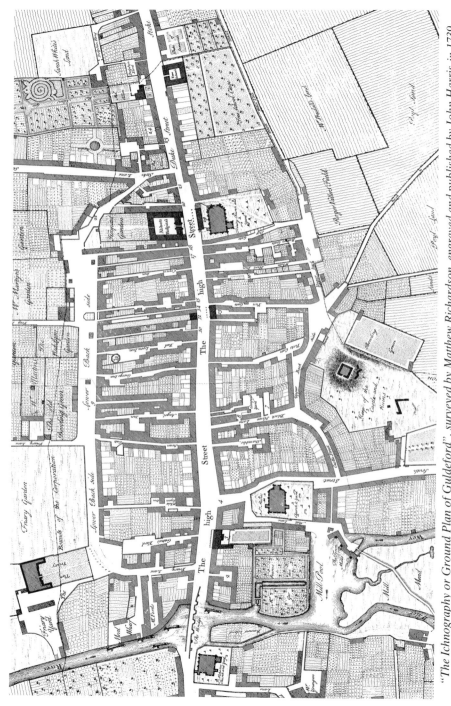

"The Ichnography or Ground Plan of Guldeford", surveyed by Matthew Richardson, engraved and published by John Harris in 1739.

GUILDFORD
A Short History

Matthew Alexander

AMMONITE BOOKS
GODALMING

Acknowledgements

My thanks to my wife Mary and to Shirley Corke for their valuable assistance.

FIRST PUBLISHED 1986
Reprinted 1992, 2001 (with revisions)
© Matthew Alexander 1986, 1992, 2001

ISBN 1 869866 02 9

Printed and bound in the United Kingdom by Unwin Brothers Ltd,
The Gresham Press, Old Woking, Surrey

Contents

For Elizabeth

Introduction

Guildford has a long history, and it is hard to write a short one. Much has, of necessity, to be left out, but the bibliography points to sources where more detail can be found. A full account of the town's history is certainly needed, but it will be the product of a lifetime's research.

I trust this small volume will fulfil a need, however. Interest in local history is growing, perhaps because the rate that things change is increasing, and Guildford, a major town for over a thousand years, is particularly rewarding to study.

Matthew Alexander

I. Origins and the Saxon Settlement

To understand the origins of Guildford we must look back long before human beings walked the earth. During the Cretaceous period – beginning some 135 million years ago – the successive layers of sediments were laid down which were to form the geological structure of southern Surrey. For much of the time, the present-day county was under water and was at first covered by a freshwater lake. The mud that settled on the bottom of this lake became the Weald clay. Then the sea flooded over the area, depositing layers of sand – the Lower and Upper Greensands. The creamy ooze that subsequently formed on top of the sea bed was composed of the skeletal remains of untold millions of minute creatures which lived and died in that sea. The ooze solidified into chalk, in which the remains of many of the larger creatures were preserved as fossils.

About 25 million years ago, earth movements raised south-east England above sea-level, forming the dome known as the Wealden anticline. Now exposed to the elements, the chalk on top of the dome was eroded away, leaving only the edges: the chalk ridges of the North and South Downs. The area north of the Downs had become part of the estuary of a huge river, depositing the mud and sand that now forms the London clay and the sandy heaths.

The rain that fell on the northern side of the Wealden dome ran off northwards into this estuary, forming streams and rivers as it went. In particular, the river we now call the Wey gradually wore away a gap in the North Downs as it flowed towards what later became the Thames. It was in this gap, and because of this gap, that the town of Guildford was to grow.

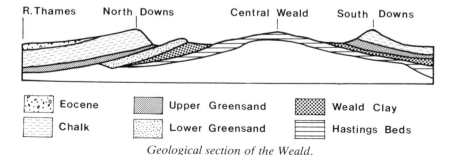

Geological section of the Weald.

9

It seems clear, however, that there was no prehistoric settlement of any importance in the gap. Flint tools from the Middle and New Stone Ages (9000–1700 B.C.) have been found on the sand ridge to the south, and here too the major Bronze Age and Iron Age finds have been made. On the other hand, it may have been as early as the New Stone Age that the trackway along the crest of the North Downs was established, fording the River Wey in the gap. It was this ford which was to give the town its name.

It is surprising that there is no evidence of a Roman town. Since A.D. 43 the Roman way of life had been increasingly adopted in Britain, and a number of villas had been built in Surrey, including one at Broad Street Common. Early Roman cremation urns have been found at Tyting and Merrow Downs. Nevertheless, despite its key location as a pass through the Downs and an established river crossing, the Wey gap did not attract a Roman road or settlement in the way that the Mole gap further east did.

The first true Guildfordians were Anglo-Saxons, migrants from north-western Europe who spoke a Germanic language from which our modern English has descended. Their first settlements in Surrey were in the north-east, south of London, and they probably came as mercenary soldiers to assist the Romano-British. Soon afterwards, in the early 400s, the Romans withdrew from Britain and many more Anglo-Saxons flooded in. They landed on the east coast and moved inland along the Roman roads and the rivers – possibly including the Wey. Those who came first claimed the best settlement areas and so later arrivals had to move further and further west to find sites equally good. This westward expansion was halted in about A.D. 500 when Arthur defeated the

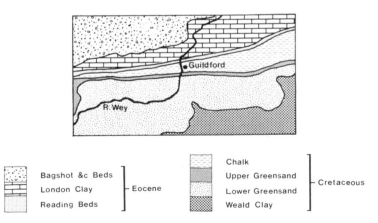

The geology of the Guildford area.

10

Anglo-Saxons at Mount Badon. Following this, the immigrants could only settle in areas already under their control – such as the rather infertile soils of west Surrey. The name "Surrey" derives from "Suthrige", the Southern district, and the area seems to have been subordinate to some tribe north of the Thames. Surrey fell awkwardly between the Jutes of Kent and South, East and West Saxons, though Wessex seems to have had the dominant influence.

It was probably at this time, the early 500s, that the first settlers came to what they called "Gyldeforda" – the Golden Ford. It has been suggested that yellow flowers at the riverside prompted the name: more probably it was the golden sand of the river bed itself. The original Saxon town would have been a cluster of rectangular wooden huts, but it is by no means certain exactly where it stood. It is possible that it lay at first on the west bank of the ford, but as the town grew the centre shifted to the east bank, around St. Mary's. What is certain, though, is that those early Guildfordians buried their dead in a cemetery on the Mount, the western slope of the gap in the Downs. In 1929 archaeologists unearthed thirty-five skeletons dating from the 6th century, together with many of the objects with which they were buried. At this time the Saxons were pagans, believing amongst other things that anything buried in the grave with the body would accompany the soul to heaven. Some were buried with their spears, several had sheath-knives at their belts, others had pots that would have contained food and drink. Two men had fine glass beakers with them, conical drinking vessels which could only be set down when empty. All would have been fully dressed, many with rings, bead necklaces and the brooches which were used to fasten clothing.

During the middle of the 7th century, missionary priests probably from Winchester succeeded in converting the pagan Saxons to Christianity. It is unlikely that Guildford was an important settlement at this date, for these missionaries seem to have been based at Stoke, rather than in the town itself. The Guildfordians ceased to bury objects with their dead, and it may be around this time that a small wooden church was first built on the site of St. Mary's.

Guildford first appears in written records in the 880s, when Alfred the Great's will left his royal residence there to his nephew Aethelwald. Its location is unknown, and a royal residence would not itself imply a major town. Indeed, at this time the west Surrey "burh", a fortified refuge from Danish attacks, was at Eashing near Godalming. It was in the early 900s that Guildford began to develop as the major defensive and commercial centre for west Surrey. It was probably at this time that the town was greatly enlarged. A boundary ditch was dug along what became Friary Street, North Street and down the line of Castle Street to the earlier settlement around St. Mary's. This enclosed an area of land on either side

11

The site of the Golden Ford – the Town Bridge in 1904.

of what became the High Street. The land was divided up into long, narrow plots, enabling houses to be built on the street with long, narrow yards or gardens to the ditch at the rear. This was quite deliberate town planning and, if we were to look at Totnes in Devon, we would see an almost identical pattern. If we can take Totnes as a parallel, then we might guess what happened at Guildford. Edward the Elder, who reigned from 899 to 924, may have replaced the ford with a wooden bridge: not so much to cross the river as to block it, preventing Danish raiding parties coming upstream in boats. At the same time the town was enlarged as a base against the intruders.

Whether or not this was the case at Guildford, by the mid 10th century the town was the commercial centre of west Surrey. This is demonstrated by the mint which was set up in the town in the reign of Edward the Martyr (975–979). Southwark had the only other mint in Surrey, and the fact that Guildford had this privilege of striking the royal coinage indicates that it had the status of a "borough".

In 1036 there occurred what was almost the only event of national importance to have taken place in Guildford, an event which reflects little credit on the town. The tale is told that Alfred the Atheling, younger brother of Edward (later King Edward the Confessor) came to England

12

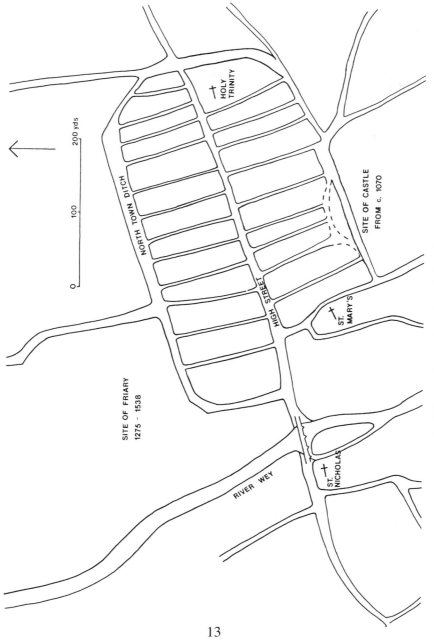

HOLY TRINITY

NORTH TOWN DITCH

SITE OF CASTLE FROM c. 1070

HIGH STREET

ST. MARY'S

SITE OF FRIARY 1275 – 1538

RIVER WEY

ST. NICHOLAS

200 yds

100

0

Guildford as it may have been in late Saxon times.

13

from Normandy and was greeted with apparent friendliness by Godwin, Earl of Wessex. He and his entourage were escorted by Godwin's soldiers to Guildford, but after a convivial feast, Godwin's men rose up in the night and brutally murdered the Atheling's companions. He himself was blinded and died in captivity. The revulsion that followed the news of this massacre was due not so much to its cruelty but to the scandalous breach of the tradition of hospitality. There are confusing and conflicting accounts of the affair, but the discovery of nearly two hundred mutilated skeletons on the Mount may confirm the basis of the story. On the other hand, the discovery of a coin of about 1043 with one of the skeletons suggests that some, at least, may be the remains of criminals executed later.

In about 1050, the wooden church of St. Mary's was rebuilt in stone, and its tower is the oldest building in the town, the only surviving part of Saxon Guildford. It very probably stood at first at the west end of a small church, topped with a wooden belfry which was later replaced by battlements. The shallow pilaster strips and the small double-splayed windows which are characteristic of Saxon building can still be seen in the chalk and flint rubble walls.

Abandoning strict chronology for a while, let us examine the history of St. Mary's down to the present day. In about 1120 Henry I gave the church to the canons of Merton Priory, who held it until the Reformation. It was probably at this time that St. Mary's was enlarged. Two transepts were added to the north and south of the tower, and arches opened into them through the tower walls. The east end was rebuilt and very probably a small nave was added to the west of the tower, making the church cross-shaped with the tower in the centre. The site on the slope down to the river necessitated a wedge-shaped footing to be constructed to make the nave floor roughly level. In the middle of the 12th century the chancel was again reconstructed and two side chapels with rounded ends or "apses" added, St. John's to the north and St. Mary's to the south. Side aisles were added to the nave, with typically massive Norman pillars supporting pointed arches in the newer "Early English" style. Ribbed stone vaulting was added to the chancel and chapels early in the 13th century and around the 1250s the aisles were extended to their present size. This was a time when Henry III was spending much time and money at the castle nearby, and it is possible that his wall-painter William Florentine painted biblical scenes and decorative patterns in St. Mary's, traces of which can still be seen in St. John's chapel.

Structurally, St. Mary's has changed little since Henry III's time, though the later Middle Ages saw the replacement of the small, early windows with larger ones. There would have been at least six altars in the church: the high altar in the chancel, one in both chapels, one at the east

14

end of both aisles, and one in front of the rood screen blocking the arch between nave and tower. A "rood" or crucifix would have stood on this, with a balcony reached by the doorway still visible high up in the wall. A small window low down at the west end, closed by a wooden shutter, may have been used to hear confessions.

The late Saxon tower of St. Mary's.

The Reformation of the mid 16th century swept away all the altars save a communion table in the chancel. The rood screen was taken down, the wall-paintings white-washed over and texts from the Bible written instead. In 1709 a gallery was built at the west end in the fashion of the time and in 1825 the chancel was shortened to widen Quarry Street. The story goes that this was to make it easier for George IV to get his coach past on the way from Windsor to Brighton, but sadly there is nothing to confirm this. In 1863 St. Mary's was "restored". The architect, Thomas Goodchild, removed the gallery but was otherwise reasonably restrained, and so St. Mary's escaped the over-enthusiasm that did so much damage to many other Surrey churches. Although the west end has housed the S.P.C.K. bookshop since 1979, St. Mary's continues today as a place of worship, as it has for over a thousand years.

II. The Middle Ages

The Normans conquered southern England in 1066 and were posed with the problem of keeping the country under their control with a comparatively small armed force. The technique they introduced was to build castles in the major centres of population: Guildford was one such. The Domesday survey of 1086 lists Guildford as the principal Surrey town, held by the king. Its population at this date was probably between 300 and 400: not a large settlement certainly, but one that warranted the building of the only royal castle in Surrey.

We do not know when building was begun, but it was probably within the first five years of the Norman occupation. (The fact that there is no reference to a castle in Domesday Book does not mean that none existed: no church is mentioned and St. Mary's was undoubtedly standing.) There is certainly no evidence of any earlier fortification at Guildford, despite the fanciful notice now displayed in the keep. The site was carefully chosen to dominate the town. A spur projecting from the hillside was cut

The castle "motte" or mound.

17

off by digging a deep ditch across its neck and the chalk spoil was heaped on to the spur to form a flat-topped mound or "motte". To the south-west a triangular "bailey" was enclosed with a ditch and very probably a wooden palisade. Within the bailey would have stood the domestic buildings housing the garrison – a band of horsemen whose presence would deter or suppress any local rebellion. If attackers broke into the bailey, the defenders could retreat behind the palisade which encircled the top of the motte.

At first the castle buildings would largely have been of timber, but over the next century these were replaced with more solid structures of stone. The palisade around the crest of the mound was rebuilt as a chalk wall, forming a "shell keep", and then in the mid 1100s, the great square tower-keep was built which still dominates the ruins. Much of its massive weight is carried on the thick east wall, which rests on solid chalk. The only entrance was at first-floor level, reached by a flimsy stair or ladder that could be destroyed or drawn up by the defenders. The walls are built of Bargate sandstone from the Godalming area, and were originally white-washed. For much of the Middle Ages the keep was used as the county gaol for Surrey and Sussex until the building of prisons at Lewes castle and in south London supplanted it. Guildford castle never underwent any major siege, although its defences were strengthened in 1173 during Prince Henry's rebellion and it was briefly occupied in 1216 by forces supporting the French Dauphin against King John. By this time it was becoming important more as a palace than a fortress.

In the bailey stood the buildings, "the King's houses", which accommodated the royal court when it stayed at Guildford, and in the 13th century Henry III made them into one of the most luxurious royal palaces in England. The great hall was the focus of the castle's life, with the richly decorated royal apartments nearby. The king had his private chapel (St. Stephen's) and the queen hers (St. Katherine's), and there were lodgings for courtiers, kitchens and so forth, with gardens in between. Following a serious fire in 1254, the king's master mason, John of Gloucester, rebuilt much of the palace. In 1256 he probably built the gateway now known as Castle Arch, perhaps using chalk from the mines, the "Caverns", leading from Racks Close.

In 1266 the castle was the scene of a picturesque incident. Henry III's son Edward had personally captured Adam de Gurdon, one of the rebel Simon de Montfort's followers, and brought him to Guildford. Prince Edward's wife, Eleanor of Castile, successfully pleaded with her husband to spare Adam's life: possibly it was all a propaganda ploy to encourage other rebels to give themselves up.

After Henry III's death in 1272 his widow, Eleanor of Provence, held Guildford castle in dower, but thereafter the buildings were neglected

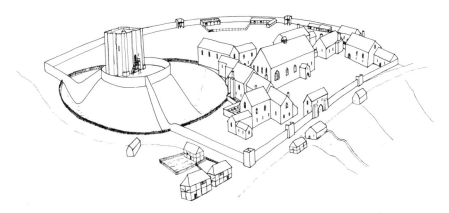

Guildford Castle as it may have looked in the 1260s.

and by 1379 most had fallen down. When royalty now visited the town, they preferred to stay in the hunting lodge in the park across the river.

In 1611 the perennially insolvent James I sold the ruined castle to a Guildford merchant named Francis Carter, who attempted to live in the keep and made some alterations in brick. However, a mediaeval prison makes an inconvenient home, and in about 1630 Carter built a comfortable new house at Castle Arch. The keep was then unroofed and used as a cockpit. The castle ditch which had run along Castle Street and Quarry Street had been filled in to allow house-building there. Subsequently the Castle grounds passed through several hands before being bought by Guildford Borough Council in 1885 to be laid out as public pleasure grounds.

By Henry III's reign Guildford had become a wealthy town and its prosperity derived largely from the wool trade. The Cistercians, who founded Waverley Abbey in 1128, introduced commercial wool production into west Surrey. The downs and commons provided rough grazing; and the sheep were shorn, the fleeces spun into yarn and the yarn woven into cloth in the villages and farms around. The new cloth would then go to Guildford or one of the other nearby towns to be finished.

The first finishing process was "fulling" – pummelling the cloth in a vat of water to produce a nap and also to clean it; fuller's earth was used to remove the natural grease so that the wool would take the dye. At first fulling was done by trampling the cloth in wooden tubs, but was then mechanised with the introduction of fulling mills where large wooden mallets, powered by water-wheels, hammered the wool. One of the

19

earliest fulling mills in England was built by Henry III at Guildford in 1251 and by the end of the Middle Ages at least four were operating in the Millmead area.

The next process was dyeing, frequently with woad to produce

The arms of the Borough of Guildford, showing the two woolpacks.

"Guildford blue" cloth. (There are records of dyehouses near the Town Bridge in Elizabethan times.) The piece of cloth, hot and wet from the dye-vat, would be hooked to racks or tenter-frames to dry evenly: there were racks at Millmead by 1394 and others gave their name to Racks Close. The nap would then be brushed up with teazels and sheared off to a smooth surface. The finished cloth, known technically as a kersey, was then ready for sale and much of it went for export to the Continent.

All the stages of manufacture would be superintended by the "clothier", the entrepreneur who would handle the sale of the finished product and reap a considerable profit. Nevertheless, this profit seems to have been thought insufficient by some.

As early as 1391 an Act of Parliament complained that unscrupulous clothiers were ruining the reputation of "cloths of Guildford" by stretching the cloth before drying. This artifically lengthened the piece, but the cloth would shrink back again if ever the customer got it wet. Dishonest stretching continued to be a problem for the next three hundred years and many blamed it for the final decline of the west Surrey wool trade.

The wealthy wool town began to acquire privileges. Although a borough since before the Conquest, the first charters date from 1257, when Henry III granted two, one of which confirmed Guildford as the county town of Surrey forever. From 1295 the borough sent two members to Parliament. A further step towards self-government came in 1366, when the town acquired the right to collect itself the fees due from it to the king. Soon afterwards the leading townsman, who had previously been called the "Seneschal" (a royal official) became known as the mayor. In 1488 another charter incorporated the borough's administrative body: the mayor and a group of "Approved Men".

Despite its wealth and status, Guildford remained a small town throughout the Middle Ages: the population was never above a thousand and more probably was nearer half that figure. Other county towns might have two or three thousand inhabitants, but Guildford's development was restricted by its closeness to London. Surrey customers could go to one of the great commercial centres of Europe rather than a county town for specialised goods and services.

The town consisted essentially of the High Street, with some houses towards the castle and around St. Nicholas'. The long, narrow plots on either side of the High Street had paths or passages running down one side to the ditch behind. These passageways were referred to as "gates" and some were used as public thoroughfares as the town ditch became a lane, especially those belonging to inns. Several gates still survive: Angel Gate is the best preserved, while Swan Lane, Market Street (formerly Red Lion Gate) and Tunsgate commemorate other, now vanished, inns.

At first the timber-framed houses that lined the High Street would

21

The undercroft below 72–74 High Street.

probably have all stood parallel to the street. Later, as the population increased, pressure on street-frontage space would have grown and many houses were built at right angles to the street. From the mid 14th century onwards the strong and finely crafted "crown-post" roof construction was used, and a number of good examples still survive in the town centre, such as the Royal Oak – formerly Holy Trinity rectory. Demand for shop frontages was such that in the later 13th century a number of semi-basement "undercrofts" were built, stone-vaulted cellars with steps down from the High Street. Two good examples survive under the Halifax Building Society and the Angel Hotel (where it is inaccurately called a crypt). The expensive masonry of these underground shops testifies to Guildford's wealth at this time, and they may be associated with the wool trade. The High Street itself acted as the general market place, and in the late Middle Ages a Fish Cross was built in the street near the Angel. This probably looked like the Chichester market cross, and sheltered the fish sellers. It proved an obstacle to traffic, however, and was pulled down at the end of the 16th century.

The borough was divided into three parishes: Holy Trinity, St. Mary's and St Nicholas' across the river (although a large part of St. Nicholas' parish lay outside the borough). In fact, each of the three parish churches separately could easily have accommodated the entire population of the town, and we can be sure that, at great festivals at least, virtually every parishioner would have gone to church. Certainly religion played a central part in mediaeval life. Laymen formed associations or "guilds" for religious (and social) purposes, such as the guilds of Jesus and the Corpus Christi of St. Mary's. Around 1200 a hospital dedicated to St. Thomas of Canterbury was built in the angle between the London and Epsom roads. This would have been a home for the poor, the aged and the sick, living a communal life under a master with regular religious observances. Quite separate was the leper hospital founded somewhere on the outskirts of the town before 1180: lepers were not permitted within boroughs. While still in existence in 1400, it would have closed during the next century when leprosy died out in England. The clergy was numerous, and included chantry priests who were paid by bequests to pray for the souls of the dead. The land left by Henry Norbrydge in the early 16th century to support a priest at Holy Trinity is still known as the Chantries.

In the 13th century a new kind of cleric appeared, the friar. Unlike monks, who prayed for the world in cloistered seclusion, the friars preached to as many people as possible, to save souls. Just as the monks sought empty countryside, the friars sought towns, and it is an indication of Guildford's urban status that it had the only friary in Surrey.

The friars "de ordine Martyrum" were the first to come, in 1260. However, their community did not last long and had probably dispersed by 1274. In October of that year Prince Henry died at Guildford Castle at the age of seven, and it is probable that his grandmother, the widowed Eleanor of Provence who held the castle, decided to found a friary in his memory. The Dominicans, "the Friars Preachers", were established before March 1275 at the north-west end of North Street. They may well have taken over the site of the earlier friary. If so, it was too small for them and Edward I, the little prince's father, granted them land to extend it.

The friary built by the Dominicans followed the usual plan, with a large church with a cloister or courtyard on one side, around which were the domestic buildings where the friars ate, slept and studied. Normally the cloister lay to the south of the church, but at Guildford it was to the north, so that the church was nearest to the town. It was one of the smallest English friaries, with never more than 24 friars in residence. The crown occasionally gave them money, but they lived mainly by begging. Their life was hard but the friars won great respect from the lay people – so much so that many wished to be buried in the friary church or graveyard rather than their own parish churches.

Royalty sometimes stayed at the Guildford friary – Henry IV paid 40 shillings for the damage done when he visited in 1403. Henry VIII had a "House of Honour" built in the grounds for his personal use, with gardens laid out by the friars around it. He signed a treaty with the Scots at the Friary in 1534 and he visited again three years later. However, the end was drawing near, for Henry VIII was determined to close down all the friaries and monasteries in England. In October 1538 the friary at Guildford was "surrendered" to the king, and the friars left to go their unrecorded ways.

The buildings were eventually knocked down and in the early 17th century a fine mansion built on the site, which retained the name "The Friary". This was in turn replaced in the last century by the Friary Brewery, whose demolition in 1974 allowed archaeologists to uncover the mediaeval foundations of the Dominican Friary and, below them, what may have been the remains of the friary "de ordine Martyrum". The dissolution of the monasteries and friaries ended a chapter of England's – and Guildford's – history.

A model based on the excavations of the Dominican friary.

24

III. Tudors and Jacobeans

The Tudor reformation of religion affected many aspects of life, not least education. The closing of the Guildford friary saw the end of its theological school, which probably taught local boys as well as the younger friars. By this time, however, a grammar school had already been flourishing in the town for a generation. In 1512 a wealthy London grocer, Robert Beckingham, died leaving lands whose income was to be used to found a free school at Guildford. He had already given property in Castle Street to the borough and it was probably there that the school was established, with a master and 20–30 pupils. Beckingham's will stipulated that prayers should be said daily for the souls of his wife and himself; this effectively made the school a chantry and when Edward VI confiscated the property of all chantries in 1547, the school had financial problems. These were partially resolved in 1551 with Edward VI's re-endowment, which provided for a master and an usher to assist him.

In 1551 a plot of land was acquired by the corporation just inside the borough boundary on what is now the Upper High Street, and two years later a new school building was begun. A large schoolroom was built,

The Royal Grammar School in 1853.

25

with a common room above and later a garret dormitory for boarders. Two wings provided houses for the master and usher, joined by a gallery which closed off the quadrangle from the street. John Parkhurst, Bishop of Norwich, left his Latin books to the school, and these were eventually housed in the gallery, chained to the bookshelves to prevent theft. The building work was completed in 1586, after considerable local fund-raising, leaving the school very much as it is today. From 1579 boys were given an elementary education in the school founded by Thomas Baker in his rye market house in front of Holy Trinity, fitting them to become apprentices or go on to the Royal Grammar School.

Grammar schools were founded in nearly every English borough in Tudor times, providing a grounding in Latin and perhaps Greek so that classical literature could provide moral instruction and the doctrines of the Protestant religion could be inculcated. The school flourished and in its first hundred years produced five bishops, one an Archbishop of Canterbury, and two Lord Mayors of London. Teaching in the upper forms was entirely in Latin and numbers were limited to a hundred boys, who paid 2d. a quarter for brooms, candles and canes. As time went on, however, fewer free places were available and increasingly the "free school" became fee-paying. It went into a decline in the 18th century, actually closing for a time, and fluctuating fortunes in Victorian times led to a complete reorganisation as a day school in 1889. The school buildings were subsequently extended, and a new block was opened in 1963 in the grounds of the former Allen House opposite the old school.

The corporation had played a leading role in setting up the grammar school, and this was not surprising. By Tudor times it had developed as the governor of the town's commercial life. The system inherited from the Middle Ages was a series of courts. The Guild Merchant met annually in the autumn to elect the Mayor, the Bailiff (the corporation's executive officer) and other lesser officials. Originally anyone who had the freedom to trade in the borough, by serving an apprenticeship or paying a fine, was entitled to attend the Guild Merchant. Increasingly, however, power became concentrated in the Approved Men.

The Bailiff had probably already served in various appointments made by the Court Leet, which was responsible for trading standards and the peaceful running of the town. The January Court Leet appointed the three parish constables, and sometimes their assistants, the five Tithing-men (Holy Trinity and St. Mary's were each divided into two tithings, whereas St. Nicholas' within the borough formed only one). The humblest of these unpaid officials were the Tasters of Fish and Flesh and of Ale.

The Court Leet that met after Easter was known as "The King's Great Law Day" and the Tithingmen presented people from their tithings for such offences as obstruction and dishonest trading. The jury included the Approved Men and other townsmen, and four Affeerers fixed the fines. A Three Weeks Court met every third Monday to hear personal actions, often for debt. Bread-making was also regulated, wheat prices being fixed and dishonest bakers fined. Other business included the fining of brewers and alehouse keepers and the enrolment of apprentices. The granting of a court of Quarter Sessions and a separate Commission of the Peace in 1603 underlined the borough's legal, as well as commercial, self-government. The Mayor became ex-officio the leading magistrate, and a Recorder, a lawyer, was appointed by the corporation.

Prominent townsmen also administered the Poor Laws which were introduced in Tudor times, acting as overseers in their parishes. The lot of the Guildford poor must have been materially improved after 1627, when the great Surrey philanthropist, Henry Smith, gave the rents of the Manor of Poyle to the town, the corporation distributing substantial sums among the needy. The manor lands included Poyle Lea, or Pewley Hill, but over two-thirds of the income came from the town mills at the bottom of Mill Lane.

Another of the town's benefactors – and the most significant Guildfordian in history – was George Abbot. Born in 1562 in a small cottage opposite St. Nicholas' church, he was the son of a cloth worker, Maurice Abbot, who like so many involved in the wool trade held strongly Protestant opinions and had suffered for them under Mary Tudor. It is said that Maurice's wife Alice dreamed that she would catch a pike in her bucket when dipped in the river, and that she would bear a son who would become a great man. In the event, George was given a free education at the Grammar School and proved a gifted scholar in the ancient languages. He went to Oxford in 1579, entered the church, and rose to become Vice-Chancellor of the University in 1600.

His skill in classical languages was used to good effect early in James I's reign, when he helped to translate the "Authorised Version" of the Bible. He gained the attention and favour of the king, who made him Bishop of Lichfield and Coventry in 1609. The following year he was promoted to Bishop of London and in 1611 the king nominated him as Archbishop of Canterbury.

Abbot was a surprising choice as the leader of the English church. While he had a distinguished academic record, he had never worked in a parish and had no support from either of the rival factions who were pulling the church apart. The puritan fundamentalists and the "Arminians" (whom we would today call "High Church") required a skilful and diplomatic leader to keep them together in the Church of England. Sadly, Abbot had none of the qualities needed and the resulting tensions contributed to the outbreak of civil war.

George Abbot, Archbishop of Canterbury 1611–1633.

Whatever his failings as a churchman, George Abbot felt a genuine love for the town of his birth. In 1619 he began building his "Hospital of the Blessed Trinity" in Guildford High Street, an almshouse where twelve "Brothers" and eight "Sisters" – single, elderly Guildfordians – could live out their days in peace and comfort. The building resembles very much one of the Oxford or Cambridge colleges Abbot knew so well. In plan it was a quadrangle from which staircases led to the residents' rooms. The entrance from the street was through an impressive gate-tower, with four ogee-domed turrets, and there were common rooms and a chapel with Flemish painted-glass windows. Other windows bear Abbot's coat of arms and a punning motto: "clamamus Abba Pater" – "we cry abba, father" or "we call Abbot father". The hospital, with its elaborate chimneys and gables shaped in the Dutch manner, is the finest example of the "Tudor" style of brick building in Surrey, though somewhat old fashioned for its date.

In 1621 a tragic accident cast a shadow over the rest of Abbot's life. While hunting in Hampshire, he killed a gamekeeper with a cross-bow. Although he was pardoned by the king, his religious opponents used this

Abbot's Hospital in 1903.

29

incident to make his life a misery, particularly William Laud, a leading Arminian whom Abbot detested and had done his best to hinder since they first met at Oxford. Abbot virtually went into retirement and though he crowned the new king, Charles I, in 1625, it was Laud who wielded the greatest influence.

George Abbot did not forget Guildford, however. The 1620s saw a disastrous slump in the demand for west Surrey's woollen cloth, threatening the livelihoods of 3,000 people – a large proportion of the local population. Abbot intervened in 1629 by building a retraining centre, the Cloth Hall, behind his Hospital. Here weavers were subsidised to produce linen material rather than wool, but the enterprise failed and the Cloth Hall became a poor house, then a school, offices, and recently Laura Ashley's.

Abbot died in 1633 and was buried in Holy Trinity church opposite his Hospital. His magnificent tomb has pillars supported on books carved in alabaster as a fitting testimony to his great learning. He was succeeded as Archbishop by his enemy Laud, whose persecution of the puritans led to an irrevocable split in the church. George Abbot had possessed none of the political skill this critical time in church history demanded, yet he was compassionate and charitable to the people of his native Guildford; as a contemporary remarked, "a better man than an Archbishop".

Religious and political tensions erupted into civil war in 1642. At first, Surrey's sympathies lay with Parliament and Sir Richard Onslow of West Clandon acted swiftly to stamp out any Royalist stirrings. Thereafter he dominated most of the committees which were set up to run the county, which sometimes met at Guildford, Onslow's "power base". Although Farnham was threatened, Guildford escaped any actual fighting. This does not mean, however, that it did not suffer. The heavy taxation levied to support Parliament's armies and the quartering of soldiers in the area became an intolerable burden on an economy already depressed by the failure of the wool industry. Bad harvests and outbreaks of plague made matters worse and, when troops continued to be billeted long after the fighting was over, the people of Surrey began to wish for a return of King Charles and traditional government. In May 1648 a statement was sent to Parliament from a public meeting at the White Hart in Guildford, urging a peaceful settlement with the king and an end to committees, taxes and quartering. The burden was somewhat lightened and little support was given to an abortive Royalist rising in central Surrey the following July.

In the aftermath of the Civil Wars, life was difficult for Sir Richard Weston of Sutton Place. He was a Roman Catholic and a Royalist sympathiser, which made him politically suspect. However, he was anxious to put into effect a pet scheme of his: making the River Wey navigable for barges from the Thames to Guildford. He had been planning this "navigation" for thirty years before the Corporation of Guildford finally obtained the necessary Act of Parliament in 1651. To carry out the work, Weston entered into a partnership which included James Pitson, a major in Cromwell's army and so acceptable to the authorities.

Work progressed rapidly. Nine miles of canals were dug to cut off meanders and twelve locks constructed. Sadly, Sir Richard Weston died before the Wey Navigation was completed in 1653. It was not the first such navigation in England but it was a long one – 15½ miles – and made extensive use of the newly introduced "pound" lock. The cost, however, was more than double the original estimate and, in the confusion and squabbling that ensued, Pitson was suspected of embezzlement. Nevertheless, the Navigation was a spectacular success. Barges could travel directly from the London docks to Guildford and the increased trade this generated greatly benefited the town. The main cargoes that went downstream were grain (particularly wheat), timber, and gunpowder from the mills at Chilworth. Chalk from the great quarries in the Downs near Guildford was shipped for building and fertiliser in the form of slaked lime. Upstream came a host of goods, and increasingly coal and imported softwoods.

At first the barges were rowed, then man-hauling and later horse-drawing took over. The early barges were comparatively small, but were wider and had a shallower draught than the narrow boats associated with the later northern canals. Because the journey seldom lasted more than a day, the Wey barges were rarely lived in and did not develop the brightly painted decoration of the narrow boats. In the 19th century the Wey barges became massive, capable of carrying 80 tons or more: many were built at Dapdune Wharf.

Disputes about ownership and finances went on throughout the rest of the 17th century and well into the 18th. Guildford continued to profit from the Navigation, nevertheless; the borough received a penny toll on every load coming upstream, in addition to the indirect commercial advantages. Indeed, the success of the Wey Navigation prompted an extension to Godalming in 1764. This necessitated the dredging-out of the ancient ford alongside the Town Bridge. The Godalming Navigation greatly improved trade in south-west Surrey, where the poor roads had frequently prevented the transport of heavy goods such as timber.

When the Wey and Arun Canal opened in 1816, Guildford had for a time a link with the south coast. Little use was made of it, however, and this, together with chronic water supply problems, led to the Wey and Arun closing in mid-Victorian times.

In 1902 the ownership of the Wey Navigation came into the hands of the Stevens family, who had managed it for three generations. Later they also controlled the Godalming Navigation, but continued them as two separate concerns. By the 1960s it was clear that the days of the commercial waterway were over and Harry Stevens gave the Wey and Godalming Navigations to the National Trust.

The Town Wharf lay just downstream of the bridge, with a yard giving on to Friary Street. In 1970 the whole area was demolished and redeveloped. Fortunately, the great treadwheel crane which loaded and unloaded the barges was carefully dismantled and re-erected near its original site. In its imposing black weather-boarded shed, it stands as a memorial to a prosperous enterprise.

The treadwheel crane, Guildford Wharf.

IV. Georgian Guildford

From the Restoration of Charles II until Regency times, Guildford led the peaceful life of a small provincial town. Throughout most of the period the inhabitants did not number as many as two thousand, and the town existed primarily as a market centre for local agriculture. In 1686 there was a minor municipal crisis when James II revoked all earlier charters and enforced a new one which empowered him to dismiss any member of the corporation who displeased him. He cancelled this charter two years later, just before he was driven out of the country, and Guildford gratefully returned to its old way of government.

Most of the buildings in the town were timber-framed, and had been built in Jacobean and Tudor times, or even earlier. When this style went out of favour many had new façades added, imitating in plaster and wood the fashionable classical architecture of Georgian times. Good examples of this can be seen in Quarry Street, notably in houses on either side of Rosemary Alley, and many timber-framed buildings survive behind later building in the High Street.

In the year of the Restoration, 1660, a lawyer named John Child built himself a fine new house. It was the first truly classical building in Guildford, with pilasters supporting a heavy cornice which hid the roof from view. Inside there were fine plaster ceilings and a magnificent carved staircase. Although new in design, Child's house was traditional in construction: the unfashionable oak framing was concealed behind plaster at the front and cleverly designed "mathematical" tiles at the back which imitated brickwork. The house later became a shop and eventually, in 1959, the Guildford House Art Gallery.

In 1683 the front of the Guildhall was rebuilt in an impressive style. The hall itself is Elizabethan and stands on the site of the earlier mediaeval guildhall, but it lacked a comfortable council chamber. Accordingly, one was built at first-floor level, with a balcony and a bell-turret above. Possibly as an afterthought a splendid clock was added, boldly projecting over the High Street. The story is told that a London clockmaker, John Aylward, donated the clock in return for the freedom to set up business in the borough. Whatever the truth, it was a happy inspiration, for the Guildhall clock has become the symbol of Guildford.

In 1739 the first map of the town was printed. This "Ichnography" shows Guildford to be scarcely larger than in mediaeval times. Prominent, however, are several large houses built in the red brick "Queen Anne" style. The only survivor, now sadly mutilated by inserted shopfronts, is Somerset House in the Upper High Street, built by the 6th

The Guildhall in 1925.

Duke of Somerset apparently as an overnight stopping-place on his way between London and his estates at Petworth.

One of the new High Street buildings belonged to William Haydon, a draper who found it more profitable to lend and invest his customers' money than to sell them cloth. In 1765 he transformed his business into Guildford's first bank. Acquired by the Capital & Counties Bank in 1883, the original Georgian frontage was preserved when extended in 1899. Since 1920 it has been Lloyd's.

An otherwise uneventful market day in 1740 was enlivened by the collapse of Holy Trinity church. Ill-considered alterations to the mediaeval structure caused the tower to fall, sparing only the Weston family chapel (then and now a Roman Catholic chapel) and George Abbot's tomb. Rebuilding was slow. Begun only in 1751, the rather uninspired brick edifice took twelve years to complete. Much of the cost was borne by Lord Onslow, whose crest can be seen over the clock face. The motto "Festina Lente" – "on slow" – is singularly appropriate.

Probably because of its position on the High Street, Holy Trinity was pre-eminent among the three parish churches, and here were conducted the services for civic and national events. A chancel and transepts were added in 1888 and from 1927 until 1961 Holy Trinity was the Pro-cathedral for the Diocese of Guildford.

While Holy Trinity tower was being built in the 1750s, a young boy climbed up its projecting brickwork – and was beaten by his father when

Holy Trinity, with the Weston Chapel.

35

The Town Mills in 1822.

he came down. John Russell the father was a stationer "at the sign of the Bible" and was mayor four times. His son John became an internationally acclaimed artist, particularly for his portraits in pastels. A plaque now marks the shop which was the birthplace of John Russell, R.A., the most celebrated Guildfordian of the 18th century.

Perhaps the most notorious Guildfordian was Dr. James Price, F.R.S. He astonished the world in 1782 by claiming to have transformed mercury into gold in front of witnesses who included the elder Russell. Price committed suicide the following year, however, when scientists of the Royal Society came to verify his experiments. The would-be alchemist is buried in Stoke church, his unscientific theories sadly out of keeping with the Age of Reason.

The Wey Navigation provided ready access to the great London corn and flour market. The Town Mills flourished. Occupying the same site below St. Mary's since the Middle Ages or earlier, the mills had been rebuilt in 1649, with four pairs of stones and a fulling mill. As the corn trade throve, so the wool trade declined and in 1714 the fulling mill was converted to grind wheat.

In 1701 an engineer named William Yarnold had installed pumps in the mills to supply the town with water. Pumped up hollow elm-log pipes to a reservoir at the bottom of Pewley Hill, it was fed to the consumers by gravity.

By 1768 the timber and weather-boarded mills had decayed, and by 1770 the eastern end had been handsomely rebuilt in brick. The western part was used to grind animal food until about 1852, when it too was rebuilt as an extension to the brick corn-mills. This copied its style so closely that the join can hardly be discerned.

By then, however, local corn-milling was declining as steam mills ground imported wheat at the docks. By the 1890s the Poyle Charity Trustees decided to sell the Mills to the Corporation, who had already acquired the water undertaking in 1866. They became waterworks (a plaque records the conversion in 1896) and then, in 1966, they were leased to the new Yvonne Arnaud Theatre as workshops and now as a small theatre itself.

Milling wheat was profitable, so was buying and selling it. Guildford has been a market town since before the Conquest and from the borough's point of view the corn market was the most lucrative. Housed in the front of the Guildhall itself until 1626, it moved to part of the Tun Inn opposite. In 1818 the inn was demolished and a new market house built, resembling a Tuscan temple. The portico was reconstructed as an archway in the 1930s when Tunsgate was widened into a street for motor-traffic.

Like the other markets, the cattle market was held in the High Street. In 1865 it moved to North Street, in 1896 to Woodbridge Road and finally in 1969 to Slyfield Green. In 1800 a market house for produce was opened in Red Lion Gate – soon to be renamed Market Street. This moved to North Street in 1887 and then to Woodbridge Road with the other markets. The present North Street market was started in 1919, so that needy ex-servicemen could sell produce.

Two annual fairs were also held in Guildford. The May Fair, granted in 1341, was an important livestock fair, notably for sheep and horses. The Winter Fair in November was smaller, and like all fairs both increasingly became entertainments rather than commercial gatherings. They survived as fun-fairs in the Woodbridge Road market until the 1920s.

From the routes travelled by Victorian carriers, some idea of Guildford's market area can be deduced: roughly a fan-shaped arc some ten miles to the north and another of perhaps twenty miles southwards – well into mid-Sussex. To east and west lay the provinces of Dorking and Farnham's markets.

These north and south arcs are accounted for by the road pattern in west Surrey. All roads converge on the Guildford gap to pass through the Downs, and much of the traffic from London to the central south coast passed through the town. Travellers needed rest and by the 17th century Guildford had already earned a good reputation for its inns. John Taylor, "the Water Poet," wrote in 1636 "This towne hath very fair inns and good entertainment at the tavernes, the Angell, the Crowne, the White Hart and the Lyon." In fact there were two Lions, the Red and the White, and later at least two other inns, with a host of ale-houses. The Red Lion was the largest inn, counting King Charles II and Samuel Pepys among its guests. In Victorian times, however, it declined into a pub with its "gate" re-named Market Street and closed after the First World War. The White Lion lasted until 1956, when it was demolished to build Woolworth's (this in turn has given way to a shopping arcade: White Lion Walk).

The White Hart was the grandest of all, a meeting place for county society. It was the Conservative headquarters during the rumbustious elections of the last century but it was knocked down in 1905 to build Sainsbury's. The Liberals met at the Crown opposite and during the

The High Street in the mid-18th century.

38

The Angel Hotel.

election of 1849 all the windows of both inns were smashed by rival mobs. The Crown became the National Westminster Bank: a replica of its old sign is still displayed.

Only the Angel survives. Established in the Middle Ages, it has a Tudor or Jacobean timber structure behind a Regency façade of the kind added to many inns during the heyday of the coaching trade. The archway gives on to the inn yard, where the crane to the hay-loft above the stable can still be seen.

The inns flourished as road travel increased, particularly when Portsmouth developed as a major naval base from Restoration times. At first it was a two day journey from London, and Guildford was a convenient place to stay the night. When the Portsmouth road was "turnpiked" in 1749, the improved road surface allowed a stage coach, changing its horses every 10 or 12 miles, to cover the distance in nine hours.

The turnpike trusts charged tolls to maintain the roads. There was a tollgate just south of Guildford on the Portsmouth road and from 1757 another on the Arundel road at Shalford Park. 1758 saw the turnpiking of the Leatherhead road and the Farnham road over the Hog's Back, with a tollgate on top of the Mount. The Mount was so steep, though, that an extra pair of horses had to be kept at the bottom to help pull the coaches up. Around 1800 the present Farnham road was constructed to allow a more gradual ascent.

The early 1800s saw a boom in the coaching trade. Twenty-eight services passed through Guildford, with an average of ten coaches a day travelling in each direction with perhaps 200 passengers. The inns were kept busy catering for them and changing the horses: night coaches often changed teams at the large stables at the top of North Street.

All this bustle and activity came to an end in the 1840s. The railways proved a quicker, cheaper and more comfortable way to travel and in 1849, the year the railway reached Portsmouth from London, the last coach ran through Guildford. The coaching inns lingered but they eventually disappeared, as did the turnpike trusts. A new era in the town's history was dawning.

Guildford Station in the 1860s.

40

V. Victorians and Edwardians

The railway was like a magic wand in Victorian England. Every town it touched blossomed and expanded, submerging the surrounding countryside beneath regimented rows of brick houses. The London & South Western Railway had reached Woking in 1838 and soon plans were made for a branch line to Guildford – and ultimately Portsmouth. The station was originally planned to be east of the river: more convenient for the town but needing a viaduct to cross the High Street. Fortunately a site across the river was chosen and the station opened on 5th May 1845. (The direct line to Portsmouth was not completed until 1859, ten years after the indirect route through Winchester.)

Like the roads, the railways converged on the Guildford gap, to pass through the tunnels at St. Catherine's. The L.S.W.R.'s Farnham branch and the South Eastern Railway's Reading–Reigate line in 1849 and the London, Brighton & South Coast's Horsham line in 1865, made Guildford a major junction. People found it possible to live in Guildford and go to work every day in London as "commuters", or "daily breaders" in Victorian parlance. Their importance was acknowledged with the New Guildford Line of 1885, serving commuters in the villages to the east. Guildford Station was then completely rebuilt and a "motive power depot" with a large turn-table and engine sheds constructed inside a large pit dug out of the chalk hillside.

Like the coaches, the semaphore fell victim to the railway. Since 1821 a semaphore signalling station had stood on Pewley Hill, part of a chain linking the Admiralty in London with Portsmouth. The electric telegraph which ran beside the railway was quicker, cheaper and more reliable: the semaphore closed in 1847.

The growth of Guildford began slowly, but soon the town began to acquire many of the amenities that befitted its dignity as the county town. One of these was a hospital. Surrey had none outside south London and so in 1863 the Royal Surrey County Hospital was begun on the Farnham Road. Florence Nightingale was consulted over the plans and Queen Victoria agreed that it should be a memorial to Prince Albert. Opening in 1866, it soon revealed a growing demand and was subsequently extended several times. Supported entirely by voluntary contributions until 1928, the hospital became part of the National Health Service in 1948. When the new Royal Surrey County Hospital was opened at Park Barn in 1980,

The Union Workhouse in 1838.

the old building was renamed the Farnham Road Hospital and now cares for geriatric patients.

The Union Workhouse, built in 1838, also provided medical care for its inmates, though conditions in all workhouses were made deliberately harsh to discourage paupers from becoming a charge on the parish. Matters improved though and in 1896 a new infirmary was built, becoming the Warren Road Hospital in 1930. Expanded during the war, it was re-named St. Luke's and was united with the Royal Surrey under the National Health Service.

In 1875 it was decided that army regiments should be linked to particular districts, and Guildford was chosen as the headquarters of the 2nd Regiment of Foot, "the Queen's". A new barracks was built at Stoughton and the 1st and 2nd Battalions moved in the following year. In 1881 it was re-named the Queen's Royal West Surrey Regiment but in 1959 disappeared in the amalgamation that forms the present Queen's Regiment. The Queen's then left Stoughton Barracks for ever.

Victoria's reign was a time of growth for Guildford's industries. The longest established was brewing: a good water supply, excellent hops from the Farnham area and Guildford's major corn market for barley contributed to this. At first most inns and ale-houses brewed their own beer but in the mid 1700s the Skurray family began brewing on a large scale. Their brewery near the Town Wharf was taken over by W. & E. Elkins in 1819, who ran it until 1847. On the other side of the river, opposite St. Nicholas' church, was Crooke's brewery, sold to Hodgson's of Kingston in 1925 and demolished soon after the Second World War. The Castle Brewery was built on the Portsmouth Road in 1838 by Thomas Taunton: curiously enough, his son built another, the Cannon

Brewery, next to it six years later. These combined in 1875 under Lascelles Tickner & Co., which traded until 1927. Richard Elkins ran another brewery in North Street until it was bought by Hodgson's in 1890. The longest to survive was the Friary Brewery, founded by C. H. Master in the late 1860s in Commercial Road. It prospered and took over other firms, becoming Friary, Holroyd & Healy and eventually Friary Meux in 1956. Many small breweries were being taken over by big conglomerates, not for their brewing capacity but for their tied public houses. Friary Meux succumbed to this process, and the last beer was brewed in Guildford in 1969.

Victorian and Edwardian Guildford was very much a beer-drinking as well as a beer-producing town. Throughout most of the last century there were over thirty pubs in the High Street alone.

The Guildford Foundry had been set up in 1794 near the Town Mills by Filmer & Williams, who made iron castings of all descriptions. The firm prospered by supplying the Portsmouth railway, and its structural iron-work can still be seen in many Guildford buildings. The foundry reached its peak of prosperity under the firm of Filmer & Mason from 1854–1883, and expanded by opening the Church Acre Ironworks in Leapale Lane in 1868. Dozens of items were manufactured, including waterwheels to power fixed farm machinery or to pump water for private estates such as Clandon Park. However, the great industrial towns of the north were able to mass-produce such goods at cheaper rates and local foundries declined. Filmer & Mason sold the Church Acre works in 1880 and the Millmead foundry three years later, becoming simply retail ironmongers. The two iron works passed through the hands of several engineering firms until they eventually closed, Church Acre in 1927 and the Millmead foundry in 1941.

The railway attracted entrepreneurs to Guildford. One such was Joseph Billing, who built his new printing works opposite the station in 1856, in what was then known as Railway Esplanade. Billing built a house for himself – "Coverdale" – nearby, demolished in the 1950s. His firm flourished, particularly by printing Bibles in a host of different languages for the British & Foreign Bible Society. The works had to be enlarged several times until 1962, when Billings moved to a new factory further down Walnut Tree Close. The firm has now closed and the old works have been renovated as offices.

Apart from Billings there were several other printers in Victorian Guildford, and another arrived in 1885 when Charles Biddle set up shop on the corner of Martyr Road and Haydon Place. At first Biddles handled the varied work of jobbing printers but later specialised in book production. Extensions were built and other premises acquired as trade grew: from 1922 until 1964 Biddles had a shop in the Upper High Street, at first opposite the Grammar School, then adjacent to it, and in 1923 the main building in Martyr Road was constructed. The firm continues today with over a hundred years of experience behind it.

Guildford's largest manufacturing business had small beginnings. In 1895 John and Raymond Dennis opened "The Universal Athletic Stores" at 94 High Street, assembling and selling bicycles. Experimental motorised tricycles were given publicity in 1898 when John Dennis was charged with "driving furiously" up the High Street at 16 m.p.h. – an impressive testimony to the vehicle's power. Demand grew more than the small workshop could satisfy and a building in the old Militia Depot at the bottom of North Street was used while a new works was built in Onslow Street. Later known as Rodboro Buildings, this was probably the first purpose-built car factory in England. The Dennis worm-gear transmission of 1903 proved popular and the firm turned increasingly to commercial vehicles. A new works was begun at Woodbridge Hill in 1905, turning out lorries, buses and fire engines. The First World War brought an army contract for seven thousand lorries and the factory was greatly enlarged. Dennis Brothers became a major employer and bought 21 acres nearby in 1934 for workers' housing at "Dennisville". Churchill tanks were produced during the last war but the thirty years following saw a decline in the firm's fortunes. Only a small remnant, Dennis Specialist Vehicles, survives at Woodbridge: the great factory was largely demolished in 1986.

In 1896, the year after the Dennis's, the Drummond brothers Frank and Arthur set up their engineering business at Pink's Hill. Within a few years they moved to larger premises at Rydes Hill, producing machine

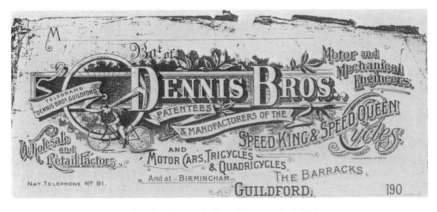

Letterhead of Dennis Brothers, early 1900s.

44

tools. Their four-inch model engineering lathe was a best-seller and Royal Naval ships were regularly equipped with Drummond lathes. Again like Dennis Brothers, Drummonds were hard hit by the economics of the 1970s and closed in 1981.

The most characteristically Victorian buildings, however, were not factories but chapels. Guildford had a strong nonconformist tradition, the Quakers and the Baptists being long established, and the Victorian age saw a revival in all religious denominations. The Methodists built their church on the corner of Woodbridge Road in 1844, rebuilding fifty years later with a finely-proportioned spire. The Congregational chapel was moved to North Street from Chapel Street in 1863, built, like the Methodist church, in Bargate stone. Other chapels were of brick, such as the Old Baptist chapel at the end of Tunsgate, rebuilt in 1860, but even the plainest were in the all-pervading "Gothic" style. St. Joseph's Roman Catholic church, rebuilt in Chertsey Street in 1881, was in the full Gothic tradition but recently it has been replaced with an office block, a new church being built in Foxenden Quarry. As town-centre sites became increasingly valuable in post-war Guildford, one by one the chapels were sold for redevelopment and moved to modern buildings further out.

The most imposing of the Gothic revival churches still stands, though, just west of the Town Bridge. St. Nicholas was rebuilt not once but twice during the last century. A church had stood there since the Middle Ages but was liable to flood. It was knocked down in 1836, leaving only the family chapel of the Mores of Loseley, and a new church erected. This proved to be cramped, dark and badly built – so much so that in 1874 it was itself demolished. St Nicholas' nearly suffered then the fate of the chapels in recent times, for it was planned to move it to the Portsmouth road. The parishioners, though, insisted on the original site. The architect was Samuel Teulon and his new St. Nicholas' was designed in his characteristically massive and sombre style. Sadly he did not live to see his work completed – and neither did its instigator, the Rev. Dr. John Monsell. Appointed rector in 1871, Monsell was a noted hymn-writer, and his works included "Fight the good fight". While inspecting the progress of the new building, he was injured in a fall and died in 1875. The new church was consecrated the following year and from 1880 was known as "St. Nicolas".

Another clergyman who will forever be associated with Guildford was the Rev. Charles Lutwidge Dodgson, better known by his pen-name of "Lewis Carroll". He first came to Guildford in 1868, three years after publishing "Alice in Wonderland", and acquired the lease of the Chestnuts, Castle Hill. This became the home of his six unmarried sisters, the last of whom stayed there until 1920. While Dodgson actually lived at Christ Church College, Oxford, he always spent Christmas and fre-

St. Nicholas Church in the 1860s.

quently parts of other vacations at Guildford. He would occasionally preach at St. Mary's and was a frequent visitor to little Miss Edith Haydon, who lived next door to the Chestnuts. He would go for long walks, often over the Hog's Back to Farnham, and on one of these the last line of "The Hunting of the Snark" came into his head.

It was while he was spending Christmas at Guildford that the 65-year-old Dodgson caught influenza and died in January 1898. He is buried in the Mount Cemetery across the river, in a rather plain and unassuming grave for one who was, and is, one of the best-loved authors in the world.

There was a new awareness of education as well as religion. Anglican and nonconformist schools were set up, together with many private schools, and after 1870 each parish had a school. Adult education was provided from 1834 by institutions which finally combined in 1891 as the Guildford Institute, with a new headquarters in Ward Street.

A turning point in Guildford's history was reached in 1836, when the Approved Men were replaced by a democratically elected Borough Council under the Municipal Corporations Act of 1835. Party politics were established on religious lines, nine Anglican Tory councillors and three Liberal nonconformists being elected. All but one, however, had been members of the old corporation.

Almost the first act of the new council was to organise a police force, with a station in Tunsgate. When the Surrey Constabulary was formed in 1851 with a station in Woodbridge Road, the two forces were briefly amalgamated. The greatest challenge to the police was the annual Bonfire Night riot of the Guildford Guys, who regularly built a fire in the High Street. Growing more violent during the 1850s, the Guys were finally suppressed in 1864. A new police station was built in North Street in 1893, though derided as "Peeler Mansion" by ratepayers who thought the cells too luxurious.

Fire-fighting had been on a rather informal footing until 1863, when a volunteer brigade was organised, a horse-drawn fire engine purchased and a shed to house it built in North Street. The shed was replaced by a brick fire station in 1872 and the brigade became fully professional at the turn of the century. The new fire station was designed by Henry Peak,

Paving the High Street, 1868. Henry Peak is on the far right.

who had become the first Borough Surveyor in 1864. He was an architect and for the rest of the century designed public buildings and engineering schemes, as well as houses for private clients. Many of Guildford's Victorian buildings are his work. Peak also supervised the laying of granite setts (not cobbles), which remain today as a feature of the High Street. This paving cost £11,000, a major sum which involved the unusual step of borrowing money. As new streets were laid out, the Council also took over their maintenance.

In 1885 the Castle grounds were purchased for a public park. One scheme involved the demolition of the Keep, but fortunately Henry Peak's plan was adopted and completed in 1888. Other public spaces were acquired, such as Stoke Recreation Ground in 1889 and the Woodbridge Road Sports Ground in 1894. 1889 also saw the opening of one of the first public swimming baths in Britain in Castle Street, and the major sewerage scheme of 1889–1895 provided the town with one of the most advanced systems in the world. From 1895, horse-drawn vans based in the Council's depot in Bedford Road collected domestic refuse. In the same year the first council houses were built in Cline Road.

In short, by 1914 the Corporation had provided most of the amenities a civilised community needs. There is no doubt that the collective hero of Victorian and Edwardian Guildford was the Guildford Borough Council.

VI. Modern Times

The First World War brought some hardships and great social changes. In 1914 life in Guildford was essentially "Victorian": by 1918 it was recognisably "modern". Increasingly, for example, women were doing what were previously men's jobs as men joined the forces. Soldiers were a common sight in the town, from the large camps in the area. There was great excitement on 13th October 1915 when a Zeppelin dropped a dozen bombs near St. Catherine's, doing little damage and causing no injuries. The greatest privation though was food shortages. The Queen's Regiment suffered terrible casualties in the trenches, and a total of 492 Guildford men were killed during the war. Their names are inscribed on the memorial in the Castle Grounds. Somewhat curiously, a tank was parked at the bottom of North Street in recognition of the town's War Savings effort; it was scrapped in 1923 as many wished no reminder of the horrors of war. A more fitting memorial was the gift by the Friary Brewery of Pewley Down to the corporation.

Peacetime saw Guildford Borough Council once more extending its services. In 1921 it bought the electricity works which had been established in Onslow Street in 1896. This proved a highly profitable undertaking, enabling rates to be kept comparatively low. A new power station was built in Woodbridge Road in 1928, supplying electricity well beyond the borough boundaries. In 1933 the Corporation took over the running of the museum, set up by the Surrey Archaeological Society at Castle Arch in 1898.

The municipal enterprise which attracted most attention, not only in Britain but throughout the world, was the Work Fund set up by the mayor, William Harvey, to relieve the unemployed. The construction of the Guildford by-pass in 1933 enabled the Lido to be built adjacent to it, by workmen paid by contributions to the fund.

The new by-pass emphasised the growth of motor traffic through the town, and the railways also were carrying more passengers. The electrification of the New Guildford Line in 1925 and the main line in 1937 heralded a great increase in the number of commuters. Guildford was rapidly expanding, and amongst its new buildings were more cinemas. The façade of the Guildford Picture Palace of 1920 survives as the entrance to the Tunsgate Arcade. Its mock-Tudor style was unfashionable by 1935, when the Odeon was built in the "Art-Deco" manner.

By far and away the greatest new building, however, was the Cathedral. Guildford had been designated as a suffragan or subsidiary

4   49

The Mayor, William Harvey, opens the Lido, 1933.

bishopric as early as 1534, though no suffragan was appointed until 1874. In May 1927 Guildford became an independent diocese, detached from the large parent diocese of Winchester. The first Bishop of Guildford, Dr. Harold Greig, was enthroned in Holy Trinity, which acted as the Pro-Cathedral until a new cathedral could be built. A site on the top of Stag Hill was donated by the Earl of Onslow and in 1932 Edward Maufe's design was accepted. The Archbishop of Canterbury laid the foundation stone in 1936 and building commenced, using bricks from the clay of Stag Hill itself. The outbreak of war halted the work, and it was slow to resume when peace came, though the crypt chapel was dedicated in 1947. Shortage of money hindered the work, but the energetic appeals of the Provost, Walter Bolton, bore fruit and the Cathedral Church of the Holy Spirit was consecrated in the presence of the Queen in May 1961. It is a popular misconception that having a cathedral automatically makes Guildford a city. Only a royal charter can, and Guildford remains a borough.

The Second World War, unlike the First, put Guildford into the front line – or almost. In the summer of 1940 the threat of German invasion prompted the construction of the "G.H.Q. Stopline", a deep anti-tank ditch overlooked by a chain of circular concrete pillboxes all along the North Downs. It is now known that one of the German plans involved a landing on the Sussex coast that would drive northward through the Guildford gap to outflank London. Had they ever established a bridgehead, then perhaps one of the crucial battles of the war might have been fought at Shalford.

The menace from the air, on the other hand, was not merely theoretical. Some 118 bombs were dropped on the borough, damaging houses but hitting no significant military or industrial targets. The worst incident was in October 1940 when four people were killed at Rydes Hill. In May 1941, in what proved to be the last raid, a stick of bombs was dropped on Charlotteville by an aircraft which apparently mistook the hospital, with its hutted wards and boiler chimney, for a factory. There was no planned attack on Guildford, however, and the five flying bombs that fell in the summer of 1944 were strays. One exploded in the middle of Stoke Recreation Ground, the blast shattering windows over a wide area.

Units of the Home Guard, the A.R.P., and the Auxiliary Fire Service

Guildford House Gallery in the 1950s.

51

were organised and the Borough Council found itself responsible for implementing a host of emergency regulations and services. Furthermore, the influx of servicemen, war-workers and evacuees into the town prompted the council to embark on an enterprising series of cultural amenities.

The first of these was a public library, opened in 1942 in the old Borough Hall in North Street. After the war it moved to wooden huts in the Upper High Street, then to a purpose-built library in North Street in 1962. The Philharmonic Orchestra was formed in 1945, giving concerts at the Odeon and the Technical College in Stoke Park until the Civic Hall was built for it in 1962. An art gallery was set up in a shop in the Upper High Street. Known as Guildford House, the name and the gallery were transferred to the former Nuthall's Restaurant in 1959. Sports provision was enhanced when the Sports Centre replaced the Castle Street baths in 1971.

While the Borough Council was taking the initiative in arts and recreation, many of its existing functions were being taken from it by other authorities. In 1946 the Guildford Borough Police were amalgamated with the Surrey Constabulary and the Surrey County Council also took over the fire brigade the following year. 1948 saw the electricity works nationalised and four years later the corporation lost its waterworks. Similarly, the borough handed its educational functions to the county.

The theatre played its part in Guildford's post-war cultural renaissance. There had been earlier theatres: one stood in Market Street for a hundred years from 1789, and the Theatre Royal occupied the old County Hall in North Street from 1912 until 1932, when fire regulations caused its closure. However, in 1946 the Henderson brothers opened a theatre in the adjacent Borough Hall, which ran until destroyed in a spectacular fire in 1963. By that time, though, the need for a larger, purpose-built theatre for Guildford had been recognised and following a successful appeal the new building was completed on the site of the old Millmead foundry in 1965. It was named the Yvonne Arnaud Theatre after the popular actress who had died in Guildford in 1958.

Further education expanded with extensions to the Technical College, the founding of the Guildford School of Acting and Dance by Bice Bellairs in 1964 and the coming of the College of Law to Braboeuf Manor in 1967. Most significant of all, however, was the arrival of the University of Surrey. The Battersea College of Advanced Technology had outgrown its London accommodation and Guildford was chosen as its new home. Building began on the hillside below the new cathedral in 1966, and the first students moved in two years later. The newly-fledged university still retained, though, its essentially technological roots. Its site was symbolic as well as practical: Stag Hill had afforded Guildford the status of not only

52

The Cathedral of the Holy Spirit and the University of Surrey. (A.V.A. Unit, University of Surrey.)

a cathedral town but a university town as well. In 1974 local government reorganisation saw the municipal borough combined with the Guildford Rural District, which had been set up in 1888 and stretched from Ash in the west to Effingham in the east. This allowed the new borough to keep its old name, while others less fortunate were subsumed in anonymous new authorities. Nevertheless, the rural parishes preserve their identity quite separate from the town in their midst. The reorganisation also saw the borough losing responsibility for its library, highways and trading standards – the last a function exercised since the Middle Ages.

The amalgamation of 1974 was the largest of a series of boundary extensions. As the population rose, the three parishes of the ancient borough quickly reached saturation point. New building had mainly to take place to the north, in the parish of Stoke, as the Downs restricted dense development in the other directions. One of the first new estates had been Charlotteville, laid out to the south-east of the town in the 1860s by Dr. Jenner Sells and named after his wife. Terraced streets advanced steadily outward from the town centre and soon the population of Stoke overtook that of the old borough. The influx of ex-servicemen returning from the First World War exacerbated an already acute housing shortage. The result was the building of Onslow Village, on land sold at a quarter of its true value by the Earl of Onslow in 1920.

The Corporation rose to the challenge by increasing the number of council houses to the point where they form a large proportion of the total in the borough, notably in the large post-war estates such as Bellfields and Park Barn. The pressure for new housing, however, had to be balanced against the need to preserve Guildford's rural setting. The Town and Country Planning Act of 1932 empowered the Council to restrain development and one result was the purchase of the Mount Field to preserve forever the splash of green on the hillside at the end of the High Street.

Large residential estates, such as at Fairlands, Burpham and Merrow, need motor transport to carry their inhabitants to and from the town centre. Buses made housing estates possible, but it is the phenomenal growth in car ownership that has most affected the modern town. A new town-centre traffic system, beginning with Millbrook in the 1960s and the gyratory with its new bridge in the early 1970s, was an attempt to control

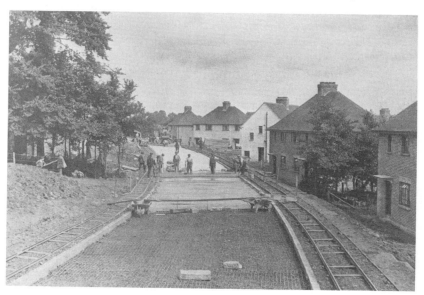

The Westborough housing estate, 1927.

54

the increasing flood of vehicles. This had the unfortunate result of cutting the High Street off from the now-redundant Town Bridge. The network of roads converging on the Guildford gap that fed the town in the past now threatened to choke it with traffic. Despite the introduction of 'park and ride' and free shuttle buses, traffic jams are still a regular problem for those who drive to work and shop in Guildford.

The shops in Guildford's famous High Street reflect the retail revolution of modern times. Old established family firms, with the tradesmen living over the shop, have been replaced by large, national chains. The town has also become a centre for building societies, banks, estate agents and other financial institutions, some moving their regional headquarters out of London to Guildford. It is worth noting that more people commute in to work in Guildford than commute out.

By the start of the new millennium, Guildford had become one of the twenty most profitable towns for business, and it is rated the top retail centre in the South East outside London. As the location of the Government Office for the South East and the South East England Development Agency, it can claim a certain pre-eminence in the region.

And what of the town in the future? Will modern trends continue, or will some new and unexpected direction be taken? These speculations are not for the historian, however. All we can hope is that Guildford, with fifteen hundred years of history, will preserve enough of its character for future generations to appreciate why William Cobbett considered the town "one of the most agreeable and most happy looking that I ever saw in my life".

Bibliography

One of the major difficulties of local history research is that so much information exists only in unpublished sources. In the case of Guildford, most of these are housed at the Surrey History Centre at Woking. There is also a large number of printed works, which offer valuable information and these can also be consulted at the Centre. The Guildford Institute has a good collection of local material and some of the titles listed below can also be consulted at Guildford Library.

Although out of date in some respects, the following countywide histories contain much that is related to Guildford and should be used in conjuction with their indexes:

Brayley, E.W. *A Topographical History of Surrey*, 5 vols, 1841
Manning, O. & Bray, W. *The History and Antiquities ... of Surrey*, 3 vols, 1804-14
Surrey Arch. Soc. *Surrey Archaeological Collections*, 1858 to date
Victoria County History of Surrey, 4 vols, 1902-1914

Books and pamphlets with specific reference to Guildford include:

Alexander, Mary *Guildford Castle: Official Guide*, 1999
Alexander, M. *The Making of Guildford Blue*, 1977
Alexander, M. *Guildford As It Was*, 1978
Alexander, M. *Vintage Guildford*, 1981
Alexander, M. *A Short History of St.Mary's Church, Guildford*, 1982
Alexander, M. *The Guildford Guildhall: A Guide*, 1988
Brown, S. J. *Dennis: 100 Years of Innovation*, 1995
Butts, M. *Recording Guildford Houses*, c.1990
Chamberlin, E.R. *Guildford: A Biography*, 1982 edn.
Chamberlin, R. *Guildford, Town Under Siege*, 1987
Clark, L. *Stoke ne. t Guildford: A Short History*, 1999
Collyer, G. & Rose, D. *Images of Guildford*, 1998
Collyer, G. & Rose, D. *Guildford: The War Years 1939-45*, 1999
Corke, S. *Guildford: A Pictorial History*, 1990

Dance, E.M. *The Borough of Guildford 1257-1957* (catalogue of exhibition of records)

Dance, E.M. *Guildford Borough Records 1514-46*, Surrey Record Soc. Vol 24, 1958

Davies, P.M. *The Old Royal Surrey County Hospital*, 1982 (also refers to other hospitals)

Green, J.K. *Sidelights on Guildford History I-IV*, 1952-6 (offprints of newspaper articles)

Haslam, J. (ed.) *Anglo-Saxon Towns in Southern England*, 1984

HMSO *London & the Thames Valley* and *The Wealden District* (British Regional Geology Handbooks)

Howell, K. *Francis Frith's Around Guildford*, 2000

Janaway, J. *Guildford: A Photographic Record*, 1990

Janaway, J. & Head, R. *Guildford Past and Present*, 1985

Morgan, G. *The Guildford Guy Riots*, 1992

Oakley, W.H. *Guildford in the Great War*, 1934

O'Connell, M. *Historic Towns in Surrey*, Surrey Arch. Soc. Research Vol 5, 1977

Penycate, J.W. *A Guide to the Hospital of the Blessed Trinity*, 1976

Poulton, R. & Alexander, Mary *Guildford's Dominican Friary*, 1979

Poulton, R. & Woods, H. *Excavations ... of the Dominican Friary at Guildford*, Surrey Arch. Soc. Research Vol 9, 1984

Poulton, R. *The Royal Castle and Palace at Guildford*, c.1996

Rose, D. *Memory Lane: Guildford & District*, 2000

Russell, J. & S. *The History and Antiquities of Guildford*, 1801 (the earliest general history)

Sturley, D.M. *The Royal Grammar School of Guildford*, 1979

Sturley, M. *The Breweries and Public Houses of Guildford*, 1990

Sturley, M. *The Breweries and Public Houses of Guildford, Part 2*, 1995

Taylor, B. *The Lower Church*, 1980 (a history of St Nicolas')

Taylor, B. *Abbot's Hospital, Guildford*, 1999

True North Books *Memories of Guildford*, 2000

Twelvetrees, R. & Squire, P. *Why Dennis – And How*, 1945

Vine, P.A.L. *London's Lost Route to the Sea*, 5th ed., 1996 (good sections on the Wey and Godalming Navigations)

Welsby, P.A. *George Abbot: the Unwanted Archbishop*, 1962

Index

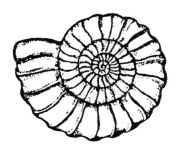

For full details of our publications please write to:

Ammonite Books
58 Coopers Rise
Godalming
Surrey GU7 2NJ